The Lover In Me

Gabrielle Holmes

BookLeaf Publishing

India | USA | UK

Presentation by *BookLeaf Publishing*

Web: www.bookleafpub.com

E-mail: info@bookleafpub.com

ISBN: 9789357612319

First edition 2022

DEDICATION

For My Family & My Friends

ACKNOWLEDGEMENT

Mom and Dad:
I would like to thank my mom and dad for supporting me throughout everything in my life. Mom, thank you for being my rock and never letting me lose sight of the things I love most in life. You have shaped me to become the young woman that I am today. Dad, thank you for pushing me to strive for excellence in everything I do and for being the best go-to person. You have shown me what it means when people say "true hard work pays off." I love you both and thank you for allowing me to have such an incredible support system my entire life.

D and Bobalini:
Thank you both for being the most supportive, loving and caring brother and sister I could ever ask for. D, thank you you for being the best role model in the world, you always

strive for nothing but the best
and I envy that. Thank you for
always helping and guiding me
in the right direction.
Bobalini, thank you for being
my shoulder to cry on and the
best little brother ever. I
can't wait to come home and
have some oodles and noodles
with you. I love you both
endlessly and don't know where
I would be had I not been lucky
enough to have the coolest
siblings in the world.

Pappy Holmes, Brian and Amy:
My Holmes family (Pappy, Brian
and Amy), thank you for
supporting me throughout my
life and staying involved.
Pappy, you have been there
since day 1 to give me a
helping hand in life. Brian,
you have shown me that it's
okay to be a kid at heart. Amy,
you helped guide me through
life with laughs and giggles
along the way. I appreciate and
love you all for everything you
have done for me.

GD and PK:
Thank you both for believing in
me and always encouraging me to
do my best. GD, thank you for
being honest with me even when
no one else was. PK, thank you
for opening my eyes up and
helping me learn to believe in
myself. I love both of you very
much.
(Hey PK, how is this for
stepping out of my shell?)

Aunt Nan, Brad, Aunt Missy:
Thank you all for being there
for me when I needed it most.
Aunt Nan, you have helped me
gain the confidence to do
anything I want in this world.
Brad, you have given me more
laughs and memories than I
could ever count, I love you
for that. Aunt Missy, you have
inspired me to be who I want to
be, do what I want to do and go
wherever I want to go. You
taught me what it truly means
to follow my heart. Thank you
all for everything you have

done for me throughout my
lifetime. I love you.

Angel:
Thank you for being my second
sister and for supporting me in
anything (even my stupid
decisions). You have taught me
what it means to be honest and
hardworking. I love you and I
am so thankful for the impact
you have left on my life.

Sar-Bear, Big Bertha, Kyla,
Nick and Sav-Dog:
I would like to thank every
single one of you for believing
in me no matter what. Sar-Bear,
thank you for helping me become
a better writer even if I was
salty about it. Big Bertha and
Kyla, thank you both for always
being there for me to complain
to and for being such amazing
and loving friends. Nick, thank
you for reassuring me that I am
not going to fail at life and
that I really can publish a

book. Sav-Dog, thank you for being my inspiration for when I am feeling down. You have all left such an unforgettable imprint on my life and I appreciate every single one of you.

Justin, thank you for supporting me and believing in me throughout this entire process. I don't know how I would have done this without your constant reassurance and support. I love you.

Elise Stankus, thank you for helping me in the writing of this book, especially with my preface and book description. This would not have been able to happen without you, thank you.

Thank you to my 6th grade English teacher for helping me find my love for writing. I would not be who I am today without the significant impact

you have made on my life. Thank
you for everything.

PREFACE

This is a book of poems. If you
picked up the book, then you
most likely know that already.
But it is also a book of
moments.

It is a book of memories, those
little slices of life forever
ingrained in our minds because
they contributed - if only a
little bit - to what defines
us. And what defines us if not
the people we love?

Chapter 1:
For The Lover

The beginning of a book
The beginning of a lover
With a big heart
And wide imagination
Follow me on my path
But feel free to stop and stare
I promise, the poems won't care
A section for the lover
The Lover In Me….

Perfectly
Not Me

Who are you if not yourself
If not the one you long to be
Who are you if you're not me
Asking myself these questions endlessly
Who am I if I'm not me
Who am I if I don't love me
Who am I if liars surround me
If good days are bad
If heartaches I crave
Who am I if I am not me
A walking myth
A physical lie
Who am I
A lie, a sham, a scam
A perfectly imperfect little old me
The one I am meant to be
Many may not love
Others will adore
Much more than I could ask
But I am me
And nothing more
Not who I want to be

But who I am meant to be
Many will try to burden me
To distinguish my fire
But I shall not fall
I will not die out
Because I am here
Because I am me
In all of my painful glory.

Loneliness

The disease I carry inside me
It's not contagious
But it's not curable
It is painful
But it's not visible
It's always there
But not always bad
It hurts inside
But I try to just laugh
I cry myself to sleep at night
But no one seems to notice
It's a battle I constantly fight
But never seem to win

This disease inside me
It's never leaving
But I try so hard
It's eating away at me
But I cannot seem to make it stop
It's really there
But others disagree
It's more of a feeling
That is eating away at me

This harsh and painful disease inside of me

It destroys my social life
But doesn't seem to care
It breaks my heart
But I try to shove it away
It's never leaving
But I wish it would
It's a life long condition
But it's so not good
I envy those without it
But I will never be them
I hardly speak about it
But it's really causing me pain
It gets worse everyday
But I am stuck with it for the rest
This disease inside of me.

Goodnight Song

"I love you a bushel and a peck
A bushel and a peck
And a hug around the neck"
I can recall her singing to me
While I was falling asleep
But in the depths of the night
She could still sense my freight

"I love you a bushel and a peck
A bushel and a peck
And a hug around the neck"
She continued singing the goodnight song
Regardless of the trembles in my breath
Regardless if I was alive
Or if I was dead

"I love you a bushel and a peck
A bushel and a peck
And a hug around the neck"
She got louder with each line
Forcing sleep upon me
Becoming the nightmare

She is the one I began to fear

"I love you a bushel and a peck
A bushel and a peck
And a hug around the neck"
As she continued with her singing
I continued with my sleeping
Yet in my deep sleep
She still finds a way to haunt me

Slowly fading away
Yet in the silence of the night
All's I can hear
"I love you a bushel and a peck
A bushel and a peck
And a hug around the neck…"

The One I Have Become

Long days
With aching heart break
Longing for love
Yet having no one
The touch of a hand
The love from a heart
Almost as beautiful as a work of art
Yet my loneliness eats me up inside
Day by day
Night by night
Fighting my inner demons inside
I sit and I cry
Not only for him
Not only for love
But for the the one that I have become
Crying alone
Weeping for those
Yet I push everyone away
Because I'm afraid
Instead I just cry
I ache in my pain
I scream in my mind

Pushing for the love that I want
Reaching for the love that I need
I fall away
Wallowing away
Deep down in the harshness
Deep down in the darkness
I surround myself in my own misery
I suffocate myself in my own pain

A Poem

A poem
For all those bad days and heart aches
The never ending pain
The days when I cannot breathe
When sadness overtakes me

A poem
For myself
Not to be selfishly taken
But nonetheless
Selfishly written
A poem for me
Because who needs anything more
When everyone else is slamming doors
I fight to keep them near
But when is the time that they will fight
To keep me here
Soaking in my misery
Drowning in my pain
I'm going insane
But I feel like I'm on cloud nine
Ready to set sail and fly

A poem
For anyone that is feeling lonely

Anyone who needs themselves
More than anyone else
A poem for the self loathing
Ignorant and rude
A poem for the selfish
A poem for you

Chapter 2:
For The One
I Love

My love
The one I adore until the end of time
The one that I will always call mine
Here is to you
Not a single person
But the idea
The thought of love
The feeling of love
Here is to you
Enjoy this section
Feel the tension
But admire its perfection
Here's to love...

One Day . . .

The love that I feel
Is so unreal
Reaching for his touch
And needing all of his love
I fight back the tears
When I come to realize
He'll never be here
Never be mine
She's already got him
So he turns a blind eye
Walking away
Into the shadows of my own self pity
I wish he saw me as pretty
He truly is all that I want
Yet all that I can't have
One day he'll be mine
And finally
My life won't be ran by the flip of a dime
He will make me complete
And she will feel all of the defeat
When I make him mine
When our love does nothing but shine

My Drug

I'm not going to lie
Every night you are on my mind
And everyday I sit and I cry
I cry for us
And I cry for our love
Fading away with every missed call
Hurting inside with every unseen text
You once were the life inside of me
The fire burning bright between us
Incomparable to others
You are the love I miss
The one to hold me up
When others brought me down
Now all that I can do
Is drag my dead body around

Aching for your love
And wanting nothing more than your touch
You are my drug
Making me high on life
Something the doctor cannot prescribe
You are the love I have needed all my life
I would hate for it to slip through my hands
And just lose it all
In the blink of an eye

So stay with me
And never leave
I know things are getting hard
Not only on you
But also on me
Push through this
For your love is what I really need
Because you are everything to me
So stay with me
Until the day I die
Until I overdose
On your love
On my drug

Come Back Home

A family of our own
That's all we ever dreamt of
But what happened to right now
And living in the moment
We used to share our hopes and dreams
And laugh about all of our great memories
You would hold me tight
And we would never fight
But life is different when you aren't here
Now I constantly live my life in fear
No more long evening walks
Or early morning talks
I miss your love
I need your love
Even when you are gone
Even when I'm not home
I reach my hand out
Grasping my phone
I start to cry out
In pain
In misery
I've let everything defeat me

Alone in the dark
I don't know where you are
Come back home to me
Because you are all I need
To put me back up on my feet
And promise me that you'll never leave
We can live in the moment
And cherish our life together
We won't worry about the future
We'll save that for later
Because right now I just need my savior
Come back home to me
Because you truly are all that I need

Happiness and Peace

A loving best friend
And a sweet shoulder to cry on
You're everything I need
All in one
And perfectly fit for me
From our long car rides
And the endless moonlight
My place of peace
My home of happiness
You are the one
The one I need
The one that everyone seeks
While you're holding me tight
I close my eyes
Breathing in your scent
Soaking up your touch
And living in your love
You're something I will never forget
My love
My home
My happiness and peace
The one I can find anywhere

Any place
And any day
The one I love
The one I need
My home of happiness
And my place of peace

Until The End of Time

Laugh with me before I cry
I already have some tears in my eyes

Love me before I die
Even though I can already see the light

Hold me tight until the end of time
My dear, have I lost my mind?

Long for me until I do you wrong
I have already loved you for oh so long

Kiss me goodnight until I fall asleep
My dear, you truly are all that I need

Cry with me until I lose it all
I'm afraid we're going to have a great big fall

Leave me be before I cannot see
My dear, look what you have done to me

Look me in the eyes before I say goodbye

I promise everything will be just fine

Need me here even when I'm gone
My dear, sometimes I just need to be left alone

Wait for me until the end of time
Darling, all that I want is for you to be mine

Chapter 3: For Those I Love

Family and Friends
And all of those that I love
The start of all
But the end of a book
Cherish this section
Embrace the warmth
And accept the pain
For my family
And for my friends
I will begin…

Time of Our Lives

Way back in kindergarten
When we were only very young
A group of strong hearted young men and
women
Were very soon to come
Breaking every barricade
And pushing every limit
Reaching for the stars
And living in the moment
The class of 2021
Our class of 2021

To our parents
More than you realize
We truly are so thankful
For giving us life
And making us grateful
For handing us toys, balls, and bats
To making a level headed player
For giving us dresses, hats, and microphones
To make a beautifully spoken actor
For handing us a pen an a paper

To make a strong minded student
You kept us involved
You pushed us to do well
And we know we've been a pain
So it must have been hard
But in the end
We all turned out pretty great
Just take a look around and soak it all in
Take in these memories and cherish these
moments
My strong, level headed, loving, caring class of
2021
We thank you once again
Our dear parents
We are truly so honored
For all of the hard work that you have done to
help us
From giving us a tough skull
And the right head on our shoulders
To teaching us the ways of life
And helping us win every battle
We gained the courage to fight things we never
expected to happen
We gained the confidence to live through harsh
restrictions
We gained the power to come together as a
whole
To celebrate in times of sadness
To rejoice in times of despair

We learned to pick our head up
And our hearts
And even after the harshest of experiences to
ever happen
We still made it

To my class of 2021
From kindergarten on we've had so many
accomplishments
And so many memories
As many are yet to come
We may cherish in this moment
We may live on in each others hearts and each
other's minds forever
Because as we continue our journey
And as we continue on this bumpy road called
life
We are looking forward to a prosperous future
We are looking forward to the light at the end of
the tunnel
So as you move on in all of your future
endeavors
Take with you all of the memories
All of the laughs and giggles
From the inside jokes at the lunch table
To the feeling of walking through the hallway
after acing an exam
From sitting in the auditorium as a kindergartner

Watching your classmates walk one by one
across the stage
To the feeling of sitting on the field
Watching our classmates do the same exact thing
Whatever the memory
Whatever the moment
Take it all with you
All that you have experienced
And all that you have done
Take the good with the bad
And learn to be the good
Spread your positivity
Love endlessly
And shine bright
For as a wise woman once told me
You don't have to like everyone
But you do have to love everyone

To my class of 2021
This is the time of our lives that we will never
forget
These are the moments that we will wish to
relive
These are the little bits of life that will go down
in history
So take a deep breath
And soak it all in
You won't get it back

But either way this truly is the best time of our
lives

Your Little Girl

Forever I will be your little girl

When hard times get tough
When you think I have no love
Just sit back and remember
I love you **{Forever}**

When sad times come about
When you start to feel some doubt
Just always remember
{I will be} here until the end of time

When your heart fills with hurt
When you think I left you in the dirt
Just always remember
The days you've spent with **{your little girl}**

And when laughter's in the air
And we're all just sitting there
Just sit back and remember
{Forever I will be your little girl}

S'mores

A chilly fall night
With all of the leaves taking flight
Crickets and a crackling campfire
The longing deep desire
The calming sounds of the night
Allow me to fly my imaginary kite
Laughing with family
Over burnt marshmallows
Dropping in more wood
To see all the shadows
Laughing with my little brother
And goodnight hugs from my mother
Cooking hot dogs with my dad
Life isn't so bad
And making s'mores with my sister
Oh how much I have missed her
Crazy to think it's only one night
We get to see the bright orange light

Sunflower

Longing for a friend
I reach my hand out
And there she is
My dearest friend of them all
The tallest sunflower in the field
With bright yellow petals
She lights up the room
Without her I'd be no one
My absolute best friend
Until the very end
She loves me endlessly
And cares for me unconditionally
I love her more than words
And the world she truly deserves
My best friend is my mother
The one I lean on the more than others
With a shoulder to cry on
Or a friend to just laugh
My mom is the absolute best

To My Best Friend On Graduation...

To my best friend
You have been here through all of the years
You have welcomed me since day one
Way back in kindergarten
When I really had no one
Lost and all alone
There we sat
One by one
You've been my best friend since way back
when
And as we sit here today
Celebrating our big day
I miss you
I miss you already
I miss your hugs
And our rants
I miss seeing you everyday
I know this isn't isn't goodbye forever
But this is goodbye for now
This is goodbye

To high school
To being so close to each other
To crying on one another
This is goodbye
To seeing you everyday
I know things are going to get hard
But I know our friendship will make it
Because it had made it through so much already
From weird elementary years
And so many boyfriends
To all our friend groups
And even our high school graduation
You are my best friend
And this is going to be way harder than we
thought
It's the simple things in life
That we will miss the most
Endless nights in the pool
Running and working out in the morning
Sleepovers
And day trips
Even you making sure there's always orange
juice in your fridge

To my best friend
Although we may have to say goodbye
I know it's not for a lifetime
To my best friend
Although we will meet new friends

You will always be my number one
My go to
My other half
The left to my right
You will always be my best friend

To my best friend
I love you always
And I'm sorry
But you're stuck with me until the very end

To my best friend
Happy graduation
The start of a new chapter
The end of an era

To my best friend
Goodbye

9 789357 612319